CELEBRATING THE FAMILY NAME OF PERRY

Celebrating the Family Name of Perry

Walter the Educator

SKB

Silent King Books

a WhichHead Entertainment Imprint

Disclaimer

Celebrating the Family Name of Perry is a memory book that belongs to the Celebrating Family Name Book Series by Walter the Educator. Collect them all and more books at WaltertheEducator.com

USE THE EXTRA SPACE TO DOCUMENT YOUR FAMILY MEMORIES THROUGHOUT THE YEARS

PERRY

Beneath the wide and endless sky,

Celebrating the Family Name of

Perry

Where winds of change and time slip by,

The name of Perry takes its stand,

A legacy that fills the land.

Through fields of green and ocean's sweep,

Where mountains rise and rivers leap,

The Perry clan, with hearts so wide,

Has journeyed far, yet still they bide.

From ancient roots that knew the soil,

They shaped their world through sweat and toil,

With hands that built and minds that dreamed,

Their futures brighter than they seemed.

The Perry name, like sturdy oak,

Bears witness to each triumph spoke,

Through quiet strength and wisdom old,

Their story in each heart is told.

Celebrating the Family Name of

Perry

Not bound by wealth or fleeting fame,

But kindness threads their cherished name,

In homes where love and laughter grow,

The Perrys plant their seeds to sow.

From dawn's first light to twilight's fall,

They hear a distant, mighty call,

To stand for truth, to give and share,

For Perry's heart is strong and fair.

Through wars and peace, through joy and tears,

They've weathered storms and banished fears,

With hope like flame that never dies,

They reach for stars, unbowed by skies.

Their voices sing of unity,

Of honor, strength, and loyalty,

With every step, they pave the way,

Celebrating the Family Name of

Perry

For future generations' day.

The Perry blood, a river runs,

Through daughters proud and noble sons,

Their legacy, a beacon bright,

That shines with never-fading light.

In halls of fame, on fields of gold,

Through whispered tales by elders told,

The Perry name endures the test,

Of time and trials—they are blessed.

ABOUT THE CREATOR

Walter the Educator is one of the
pseudonyms for Walter Anderson.
Formally educated in Chemistry,
Business, and Education, he is an
educator, an author, a diverse
entrepreneur, and he is the son
of a disabled war veteran.
"Walter the Educator" shares his
time between educating and creating.
He holds interests and owns several
creative projects that entertain,
enlighten, enhance, and educate,
hoping to inspire and motivate you.
Follow, find new works, and stay
up to date with Walter the Educator™